RENNES

TRAVEL GUIDE

2024

"Rennes Unveiled: A Journey Through Time, Culture, and the Heart of Brittany, France"

Avery Raines

TABLE OF CONTENTS

Chapter 1: Introduction...4

Chapter 2: Planning Your Trip................................. 10

Chapter 3: Getting There... 15

Chapter 4: Accommodation.....................................20

Chapter 5: Getting Around....................................... 25

Chapter 6: Attractions...29

Chapter 7: Cultural Experiences............................. 34

Chapter 8: Dining..39

Chapter 9: Nightlife... 44

Chapter 10: Shopping.. 49

Chapter 11: Day Trips..54

Chapter 12: Outdoor Activities.................................62

Chapter 13: Family-Friendly Rennes....................... 71

Chapter 14: Local Events..80

Chapter 15: Language and Local Etiquette..............87

Chapter 16: Safety Tips...96

Chapter 17: Sustainability in Rennes..................... 104

Chapter 18: Technology and Connectivity............. 111

Chapter 19: Travel Tips from Locals.......................118

Chapter 20: Rennes in Different Seasons.............. 126

Chapter 21: Conclusion.. 134

Chapter 1: Introduction

Discovering Rennes: A Journey Through Time and Charm

Overview of Rennes

Welcome to Rennes, a city that whispers tales of medieval charm, artistic vibrancy, and Breton hospitality. Nestled in the heart of Brittany, France, Rennes enchants visitors with its cobbled streets, historic architecture, and a blend of tradition and modernity. As your guide to this captivating destination, let's embark on a journey through the city's rich history, cultural tapestry, and the compelling reasons to explore its treasures in the year 2024.

Brief History

Rennes wears its history proudly, each stone and building echoing tales of centuries past. Founded in the 3rd century BC by the Redones, a Celtic tribe, the city's strategic location has witnessed a kaleidoscope of influences. From Roman occupation to the medieval era, Rennes evolved into a bustling center of commerce and cultural exchange.

In the heart of the historic center, the Place des Lices stands as a witness to the city's medieval legacy. With its timber-framed houses and the majestic Saint-Pierre Cathedral, Rennes invites you to step back in time. The Parlement de Bretagne, a symbol of Breton political history, adds a regal touch to the cityscape.

Despite facing fires, wars, and transformations, Rennes has retained its distinctive character. The blend of Gothic, Renaissance, and classical architecture creates a visual symphony that captivates every visitor. As we explore the city's streets and squares, let the echoes of history guide us through its fascinating narrative.

Why Visit in 2024?

1. **Cultural Renaissance:**
In 2024, Rennes is experiencing a cultural renaissance. The city's commitment to the arts is evident in its thriving cultural scene, with events like Festival Mythos, Les

Tombées de la Nuit, and an array of performances at Le Liberté. For those seeking a blend of tradition and contemporary creativity, Rennes is an unfolding canvas of inspiration.

2. 2024 European Capital of Culture:

This year, Rennes proudly holds the title of the European Capital of Culture. The city is hosting a myriad of events, exhibitions, and cultural initiatives to celebrate its diverse heritage. The European Capital of Culture designation brings an extra layer of excitement, promising visitors an immersive experience in Breton and European arts and traditions.

3. Dynamic Urban Development:

Rennes is in the midst of dynamic urban development, with projects like La Courrouze transforming the cityscape. Modern districts complement the historic charm, offering a vibrant juxtaposition of old and new. Explore evolving neighborhoods, where contemporary art meets centuries-old streets.

4. Breton Gastronomy:

The year 2024 is a feast for gastronomes, with Rennes showcasing its culinary prowess. From the iconic galette-saucisse to seafood delights and the diverse offerings in local markets, Breton cuisine is at its flavorful best. Discover the culinary treasures that make Rennes a haven for food enthusiasts.

5. Celebrating Diversity:

Rennes, with its vibrant student population and diverse community, is a melting pot of cultures. In 2024, the city celebrates its diversity through events, festivals, and a welcoming atmosphere. Engage with the locals, explore the multicultural influences, and immerse yourself in the unique blend that defines Rennes.

6. Preserving Heritage with Innovation:

While cherishing its historical heritage, Rennes embraces innovation. The city's commitment to sustainable practices, technological advancements, and preserving its green spaces showcases a harmonious blend of tradition and modernity. Discover how Rennes seamlessly weaves its past into a progressive present.

7. Breton Festivals and Traditions:

In 2024, Rennes invites you to participate in traditional Breton festivals that showcase the region's cultural richness. Dive into the lively atmosphere of local celebrations, from folk music gatherings to regional dance festivals. Experience the living traditions that define Breton identity.

8. **Breath of Nature in Urban Spaces:**

Rennes places a premium on green spaces, providing a breath of nature in the heart of the urban landscape. From the picturesque Parc du Thabor to the serene Parc Oberthur, discover how Rennes invites you to relax, rejuvenate, and appreciate the beauty of well-tended gardens.

9. **Ease of Exploration:**

With an efficient public transportation system, pedestrian-friendly streets, and bike-friendly paths, exploring Rennes is a delight. The city's accessibility makes it easy for visitors to navigate its enchanting streets, discover hidden corners, and embrace the unhurried pace of Breton life.

10. **Warmth of Breton Hospitality:**

Beyond the historical and cultural allure, what truly makes Rennes special is the warmth of Breton hospitality. In 2024, locals welcome visitors with open arms, eager to share their stories, traditions, and the unique spirit that makes Rennes a home away from home.

Conclusion

As we set forth on this exploration of Rennes, the city awaits with open doors and a promise of discovery. Whether you are drawn to its medieval wonders, cultural festivities, culinary delights, or the warmth of its people, Rennes invites you to become a part of its story in 2024. Join us as we unravel the layers of this Breton gem, where every step is a journey through time, and every corner reveals a piece of Rennes' captivating soul. Welcome to a city that embraces the past, celebrates the present, and invites you to be a part of its future. Let the adventure begin!

Chapter 2: Planning Your Trip

Best Time to Visit

Welcome, fellow adventurers! Planning a trip to the charming city of Rennes? Let's dive into the art of timing your visit just right. Rennes, nestled in the heart of Brittany, experiences a temperate oceanic climate, making it an inviting destination throughout the year.

Spring (March to May):
Spring graces Rennes with blossoming flowers and mild temperatures. It's an ideal time for sightseeing, exploring the city's parks, and enjoying outdoor events. Don't forget to pack a light jacket for those occasional breezy days.

Summer (June to August):
Ah, summer in Rennes – a season filled with lively festivals, open-air concerts, and vibrant street markets. The warm

weather beckons you to indulge in the city's rich cultural offerings. Make sure to plan ahead for accommodations, as this is a popular time for tourists.

Autumn (September to November):
As the leaves start to change, Rennes takes on a different kind of beauty. The weather remains pleasant, and you can experience the city at a slightly slower pace. Autumn is perfect for those who prefer a more relaxed and introspective visit.

Winter (December to February):
Winter in Rennes brings a cozy charm, with festive decorations lighting up the streets. While temperatures may dip, the city's festive atmosphere warms the soul. Consider planning your trip during the winter holidays to witness Rennes adorned in holiday splendor.

Travel Requirements

Now that we've chosen the perfect time to explore Rennes, let's talk about the nitty-gritty of travel requirements. Whether you're a seasoned traveler or a first-timer, preparation is key.

Passports and Visas:

For most travelers, a valid passport is sufficient for a stay of up to 90 days in Rennes. However, it's essential to check the specific visa requirements based on your nationality. Ensure your passport has at least six months of validity beyond your planned departure date.

Travel Insurance:

Consider the unexpected. A comprehensive travel insurance policy can be a lifesaver, covering everything from medical emergencies to trip cancellations. It provides peace of mind, allowing you to focus on the adventure ahead.

Currency and Banking:

The official currency in Rennes is the Euro. Be sure to notify your bank about your travel dates to avoid any complications with your credit or debit cards. ATMs are widely available, making it convenient to withdraw cash as needed.

Language:

While French is the official language, many locals in Rennes understand English. However, learning a few basic French phrases can enhance your experience and earn you a warm welcome.

Transportation Options

With the paperwork sorted, let's explore the avenues that will take you to and around Rennes.

By Air:
Rennes is served by the Rennes-Saint-Jacques Airport, located about 6 kilometers southwest of the city center. Several airlines connect Rennes to major European cities. Once you land, reaching the heart of Rennes is a breeze, thanks to efficient transportation options.

By Train:
For those seeking a scenic journey, arriving in Rennes by train is a splendid choice. The city boasts a well-connected railway station with high-speed trains linking to Paris and other key destinations. The train station, Gare de Rennes, is centrally located, making it convenient for travelers.

By Car:

Driving enthusiasts, rejoice! Rennes is well-connected by a network of highways, allowing for a picturesque road trip. Renting a car gives you the freedom to explore not only the city but also the charming Brittany region at your own pace.

Public Transportation:
Rennes takes pride in its efficient public transportation system. Buses and a metro line crisscross the city, providing a convenient way to navigate its attractions. Consider purchasing a travel pass for unlimited access during your stay.

With these essential tips on timing, travel requirements, and transportation options, you're well on your way to crafting an unforgettable Rennes adventure. Bon voyage!

Chapter 3: Getting There

Greetings, fellow explorers! Now that your bags are packed and excitement is building, let's delve into the myriad ways to embark on your journey to the captivating city of Rennes. Whether you prefer soaring through the skies, gliding along the tracks, or navigating the roads, there's a perfect route for every adventurer.

Air Travel

Elevate Your Adventure: Taking to the Skies

1. **Rennes-Saint-Jacques Airport:**
Your gateway to Rennes is the Rennes-Saint-Jacques Airport, located just a short distance southwest of the city center. This airport serves as a hub connecting Rennes to various European destinations. Once you land, you're a mere hop, skip, and jump away from the heart of this enchanting city.

2. **Airlines and Connectivity:**

Major airlines operate flights to and from Rennes, ensuring a seamless connection from various corners of the continent. From budget-friendly options to premium carriers, you have a range of choices to tailor your journey to suit your preferences.

3. **Airport Facilities:**

Rennes-Saint-Jacques Airport offers all the amenities you'd expect, from comfortable lounges to dining options. The efficient layout ensures a smooth transition from the aircraft to the enchanting streets of Rennes.

4. **Ground Transportation:**

Upon arrival, you'll find taxis and shuttle services ready to whisk you away to your accommodation. Alternatively, car rentals are available for those keen on exploring at their own pace.

Train Services

Embark on a Rail Adventure: Arriving with Elegance

1. **Gare de Rennes:**

For those who appreciate the scenic route, arriving in Rennes by train is a splendid choice. The city's central train station, Gare de Rennes, is a hub of activity and a welcoming entry point. The station is conveniently located, making it a breeze to transition from rail to city life.

2. **High-Speed Rail:**

Rennes boasts excellent high-speed rail connections, particularly to Paris. The TGV (Train à Grande Vitesse) offers a swift and comfortable journey, whisking you from Paris to Rennes in just over an hour. Sit back, relax, and enjoy the picturesque French countryside streaming by.

3. **Regional and Local Trains:**

Beyond high-speed options, Rennes is well-connected with regional and local train services. This provides a convenient means of exploring nearby towns and attractions, making your adventure extend beyond the city limits.

4. **Train Travel Tips:**

When traveling by train, consider booking your tickets in advance to secure the best rates. Additionally, be sure to validate your ticket before boarding, especially for regional and local trains. The charm of Rennes unfolds as you step off the platform and into the heart of the city.

Roadways and Driving Tips

Hit the Road: Navigating the Scenic Routes

1. **Road Network:**
Rennes is crisscrossed by a network of well-maintained roads, making it a delightful destination for road trippers. Highways connect the city to major hubs, offering a scenic journey through the Brittany region.

2. **Car Rentals:**
For the intrepid souls who relish the freedom of the open road, renting a car is an excellent option. Several rental agencies operate at the airport and throughout the city, providing a range of vehicles to suit your needs.

3. **Driving in Rennes:**
Navigating Rennes by car is relatively straightforward, but be mindful of the city's one-way streets and pedestrian zones. Familiarize yourself with local traffic rules and

parking regulations to make your journey smooth and stress-free.

4. **Parking Facilities:**
Rennes offers both street parking and dedicated parking lots. Consider using public transportation for inner-city exploration, reserving your vehicle for more extensive adventures beyond Rennes.

Armed with the knowledge of air travel, train services, and roadways, you're ready to embark on a seamless journey to Rennes. Whichever mode of transportation you choose, the City of Knights eagerly awaits your arrival. Bon voyage!

Chapter 4: Accommodation

Welcome to the realm of Rennes, where your adventure finds its nightly abode. Choosing the right accommodation sets the tone for a memorable experience. Whether you're seeking luxury, affordability, or a touch of uniqueness, Rennes has a plethora of options to cater to every traveler's taste.

Hotels

Nestle in Comfort: Unraveling Rennes' Hotel Scene

1. **City Center Gems:**

In the heart of Rennes lies a tapestry of hotels, ranging from boutique gems to internationally renowned establishments. Leverage the convenience of being within walking distance of the city's historic sites, restaurants, and vibrant streets. Hotel Anne de Bretagne, a charming establishment, embodies the city's rich history while offering modern comforts.

2. **Chain Hotels:**

For those favoring familiarity, chain hotels in Rennes provide consistency and reliable amenities. Chains like Novotel and Mercure have a presence in the city, ensuring a comfortable stay with the added advantage of loyalty programs.

3. **Boutique Beauties:**

If you crave a personalized touch, consider boutique hotels that weave local flair into your stay. La Maison des Armateurs, for instance, is a boutique hotel that combines Breton charm with contemporary design, promising an intimate and unique experience.

4. **Luxury Escapes:**

Indulge in the lap of luxury at Rennes' upscale hotels. Le Saint-Antoine Hotel & Spa, housed in a former convent, seamlessly blends historical charm with modern opulence. Immerse yourself in refined elegance and pampering services.

Budget Options

Savings Without Sacrifice: Navigating Rennes on a Budget

1. **Hostels and Guesthouses:**
For budget-conscious travelers, Rennes offers an array of hostels and guesthouses. Le Flâneur Guesthouse, nestled in the city center, provides affordable accommodations without compromising on comfort. These options are not just economical but often serve as hubs for meeting fellow travelers.

2. **Budget-Friendly Hotels**:
Rennes boasts budget-friendly hotels that deliver exceptional value for money. The ibis budget Rennes Centre Gare offers modern amenities at affordable rates, allowing you to allocate more funds to exploring the city's attractions.

3. **Apartment Rentals:**
Embrace the local lifestyle by opting for apartment rentals. This not only offers budget flexibility but also a chance to experience Rennes like a resident. Websites like Airbnb provide a variety of options, from cozy studios to spacious apartments.

4. **Student Residences:**

With a vibrant student population, Rennes provides budget accommodation in student residences during academic breaks. This is a unique opportunity to stay in dynamic neighborhoods, surrounded by the youthful energy of the city.

Unique Stays

Immerse in Uniqueness: Unconventional Accommodations

1. **Charming Bed and Breakfasts**:
For a more intimate experience, consider staying in a charming bed and breakfast. These often come with personalized service and local insights. La Demeure de Malouinière, just outside Rennes, offers a tranquil retreat with a touch of historical elegance.

2. **Houseboats and Floating Accommodations:**
Break away from tradition by opting for a stay on the water. Rennes has houseboats available for accommodation, providing a unique perspective on city life. Imagine waking up to the gentle sway of the river.

3. **Glamping Retreats:**

For those who seek the outdoors without sacrificing comfort, glamping retreats in the outskirts of Rennes offer a perfect blend of luxury and nature. Unplug and unwind in a cozy tent or cabin, surrounded by Brittany's scenic beauty.

4. **Historical Stays:**

Rennes boasts historical accommodations that transport you to a bygone era. Château d'Apigné, a stunning castle-turned-hotel, offers a regal stay just outside the city, allowing you to bask in the grandeur of the past.

As you navigate the diverse tapestry of accommodations in Rennes, consider the experiences each option brings to your journey. Whether it's the comfort of a hotel, the charm of a budget stay, or the uniqueness of unconventional lodgings, Rennes welcomes you to rest, recharge, and revel in its enchanting ambiance. Sweet dreams in the City of Knights!

Chapter 5: Getting Around

As you lace up your exploratory shoes, let's navigate the charming streets of Rennes. Getting around this city, steeped in history and culture, is an adventure in itself. From the efficiency of public transportation to the simple joys of strolling and biking, every path leads to discovery.

Public Transportation

Embark on Effortless Journeys: Rennes' Public Transit Secrets

1. **Bus Network**:
Rennes boasts a well-organized bus network that crisscrosses the city and its outskirts. The STAR network operates a fleet of buses, ensuring accessibility to key attractions. Grab a bus map, plan your route, and hop aboard to effortlessly traverse the city's diverse neighborhoods.

2. **Metro**:

For a swift and streamlined commute, the Rennes Metro is your ticket to navigating the urban landscape. The single metro line efficiently connects major points within the city. It's a quick and reliable option, especially during peak hours when you want to bypass traffic.

3. **Bicycle Rentals:**
Embrace the eco-friendly spirit of Rennes by exploring the city on two wheels. Vélo STAR, the city's bike-sharing program, offers an affordable and convenient way to pedal through the streets. With dedicated bike lanes and bike-friendly urban planning, cycling becomes a joyous affair.

4. **Tickets and Passes:**
Optimize your public transit experience by purchasing tickets or passes. A single ticket covers both buses and the metro, making it seamless to switch between modes of transport. Daily or weekly passes provide unlimited travel, allowing you to explore without constraints.

Walking and Biking

Wander and Wheel: Embracing the Pace of Rennes

1. **Strolling Through History:**

Rennes' city center is a pedestrian paradise, inviting you to wander at your own pace. Meander through the cobbled streets, adorned with medieval buildings and bustling boutiques. Place des Lices, the central square, beckons you to explore its lively market and savor the charm of street-side cafes.

2. **Biking Bliss:**

Biking enthusiasts will find Rennes to be a haven of bike-friendly infrastructure. Dedicated bike lanes wind through the city, offering a safe and scenic route for cyclists. Rent a bike, embark on the "Circuit Vert" (Green Circuit), and discover Rennes at a leisurely pace.

3. **Parc du Thabor:**

Escape the urban hustle by venturing into Parc du Thabor, a verdant oasis in the heart of Rennes. Stroll along its manicured pathways, revel in the fragrance of blooming flowers, and find serenity by the pond. It's a haven for both walkers and bikers seeking a nature-infused retreat.

4. **Guided Walking Tours:**

For a deeper understanding of Rennes' history and culture, consider joining a guided walking tour. Knowledgeable guides lead you through hidden gems, sharing anecdotes and insights that breathe life into the city's narrative. Whether it's a historical tour or a gastronomic adventure, walking tours unveil the soul of Rennes.

5. **Walking Etiquette:**
As you amble through the streets, immerse yourself in the local walking etiquette. Rennes residents appreciate a relaxed pace, allowing you to absorb the ambiance and engage in the warmth of the community. Embrace the art of strolling, and you'll uncover the city's nuances at every turn.

In Rennes, every step and pedal rotation unfurls a new chapter of discovery. Whether you opt for the efficiency of public transit or relish the unhurried pace of walking and biking, the city welcomes you to explore its nooks and crannies. So, lace up those shoes, grab a bike, or board a bus – your Rennes adventure awaits!

Chapter 6: Attractions

As we step into the heart of Rennes, let the tales of history, the wonders of museums, and the tranquility of parks and gardens weave the fabric of your exploration. The city unfolds like a storybook, with each attraction inviting you to become a part of its narrative.

Historic Sites

Journey Through Time: Rennes' Tapestry of History

1. **Parlement de Bretagne:**

At the heart of Rennes stands the Parlement de Bretagne, a testament to the city's rich history. This 17th-century building served as the seat of Brittany's judicial power. Admire its elegant façade, adorned with intricate sculptures, and step into its grand chambers to feel the echoes of legal debates that once resounded within.

2. **Rennes Cathedral:**

As you wander through the historic center, the Rennes Cathedral, dedicated to Saint Peter, stands as a majestic beacon. Marvel at its Gothic architecture and step inside to witness the awe-inspiring stained glass windows. The cathedral's tranquil ambiance offers a respite from the vibrant energy of the city.

3. Place des Lices:

The heart of Rennes beats at Place des Lices, a lively square brimming with history. Once a medieval tournament ground, it now hosts one of the city's most vibrant markets every Saturday. Immerse yourself in the bustling atmosphere, savoring local delicacies and engaging with merchants.

4. Portes Mordelaises:

Transport yourself to the medieval era by passing through the Portes Mordelaises, the remnants of the city's ancient fortifications. These gates, flanked by towers, stand as guardians to Rennes' past. As you stroll through, envision the city as it once was, with cobblestone streets and bustling markets.

Museums

Glimpses of Art and Knowledge: Rennes' Museum Haven

1. **Musée des Beaux-Arts:**

For art enthusiasts, the Musée des Beaux-Arts beckons with an impressive collection spanning from the 14th to the 21st century. Delight in masterpieces by renowned artists, from Rubens to Picasso. The museum's diverse exhibits ensure a visual journey through the evolution of artistic expression.

2. **Espace des Sciences:**

Science enthusiasts, rejoice! The Espace des Sciences invites you to explore the wonders of the universe through interactive exhibits. From astronomy to physics, this science center fosters curiosity and discovery. It's an engaging destination for both adults and young explorers.

3. **Musée de Bretagne:**

Immerse yourself in the cultural tapestry of Brittany at the Musée de Bretagne. This museum traces the region's history, folklore, and traditions through captivating exhibits. Walk through time, from prehistoric artifacts to modern-day cultural phenomena, gaining a deeper understanding of Brittany's identity.

4. La Criée Centre for Contemporary Arts:

For those captivated by contemporary art, La Criée is a haven of innovation. This cultural space hosts rotating exhibitions, performances, and artistic events, showcasing the dynamic creativity of modern artists. Step inside and let the avant-garde spirit of Rennes unfold before your eyes.

Parks and Gardens

Nature's Symphony: Rennes' Tranquil Retreats

1. Parc du Thabor:

Step into a botanical haven at Parc du Thabor, a sprawling park in the heart of the city. Stroll through lush greenery, admire vibrant flowerbeds, and find serenity by the reflection pond. The Thabor's diverse landscapes create a peaceful escape, inviting you to unwind amid nature's embrace.

2. Jardin Saint Georges:

Nestled near the Rennes Cathedral, Jardin Saint Georges offers a tranquil oasis with its neatly manicured lawns and charming pathways. Take a leisurely walk, find a quiet bench, and revel in the harmonious coexistence of urban life and natural beauty.

3. Le Bois de Lormandière:

Venture beyond the city center to Le Bois de Lormandière, a forested area that feels like a world apart. This nature reserve is perfect for hiking or a contemplative stroll. Breathe in the fresh air, listen to the rustle of leaves, and connect with the natural rhythms of Rennes.

4. Les Gayeulles Park:

For those seeking a blend of recreation and nature, Les Gayeulles Park is a vast expanse offering sports facilities, wooded areas, and even a lake. Whether you're into jogging, picnicking, or simply basking in the outdoors, this park caters to a variety of leisurely pursuits.

In Rennes, every attraction narrates a unique chapter of the city's story. From the echoes of ancient parliaments to the brushstrokes of contemporary artists, and the tranquil whispers of nature, let each visit unveil a new layer of this enchanting destination. Bon voyage through the wonders of Rennes!

Chapter 7: Cultural Experiences

As we dive into the vibrant cultural tapestry of Rennes, be prepared to immerse yourself in a kaleidoscope of experiences. From the spirited beats of local festivals to the captivating world of arts and performances, Rennes invites you to be a part of its lively cultural symphony.

Local Festivals

Celebrate with the Locals: Rennes' Festive Spirit Unleashed

1. **Les Tombées de la Nuit**:
Kickstarting our cultural journey is Les Tombées de la Nuit, a festival that transforms Rennes into a stage for creativity and expression. This multidisciplinary event features theater, dance, music, and visual arts, taking place across the city. Let the streets come alive with performances that defy conventions and spark the imagination.

2. **Festival Yaouank:**

For those captivated by the rhythms of traditional Breton music and dance, Festival Yaouank is a must-attend. This lively event celebrates Breton culture with a focus on fest-noz, a traditional dance festivity. Join the joyous crowd, sway to the melodies, and witness the vibrant colors of traditional costumes.

3. **Travelling, Rennes Métropole's Street Arts Festival:**

Prepare to be enchanted by the unexpected as Travelling, Rennes Métropole's Street Arts Festival, unfolds across the city. Street performers, visual installations, and interactive experiences turn Rennes into a canvas of creativity. Wander through the streets and squares, where every corner holds a surprise waiting to captivate your senses.

4. **Trans Musicales de Rennes:**

Music enthusiasts, rejoice! Trans Musicales de Rennes is a renowned festival that showcases emerging talent across various genres. From indie to electronic, this event introduces you to the sounds of tomorrow. Join the eclectic crowd and let the music carry you into the heart of Rennes' dynamic music scene.

Arts and Performances

The Stage is Set: Rennes' Artistic Odyssey

1. **Théâtre National de Bretagne (TNB):**
Embark on a theatrical journey at the Théâtre National de Bretagne (TNB), where drama and performance take center stage. This cultural institution hosts a diverse array of plays, from classical masterpieces to avant-garde productions. Immerse yourself in the world of storytelling, where every performance is a portal to different realms.

2. **Opéra de Rennes:**
For lovers of classical music and opera, Opéra de Rennes is a haven of refined performances. The grandeur of this historic venue complements the exquisite musical productions that grace its stage. Attend a captivating opera or symphony, and let the melodies transport you to a world of elegance and artistry.

3. **La Crieée – Centre Dramatique National de Bretagne:**
Dive into the contemporary theater scene at La Criée, a center dedicated to dramatic arts. This cultural hub explores

innovative approaches to storytelling and performance. Attend a thought-provoking play or engage in discussions and workshops that foster a deeper connection to the world of theater.

4. **Les Champs Libres:**

Les Champs Libres is a cultural complex that houses the Musée de Bretagne, the Espace des Sciences, and the Bibliothèque de Rennes Métropole. Beyond its educational facets, Les Champs Libres hosts a variety of cultural events, from art exhibitions to literary gatherings. Immerse yourself in the intellectual and artistic ambiance of this multifaceted space.

Tips for Cultural Immersion

1. **Embrace Local Customs:**

- As you participate in festivals and attend performances, take a moment to observe and embrace local customs. Whether it's joining in traditional dances or appreciating the intricacies of Breton art, immersing yourself in local practices enhances the authenticity of your cultural experience.

2. **Try Regional Cuisine:**
   - No cultural exploration is complete without savoring the local flavors. As you attend festivals and performances, indulge in regional cuisine available at food stalls or nearby eateries. Breton crepes, cider, and seafood are just a taste of the culinary delights awaiting you.

3. **Connect with Locals:**
   - Strike up conversations with locals during cultural events. Their insights and stories add a personal touch to your experience, providing a deeper understanding of Rennes' cultural heritage. Don't hesitate to ask for recommendations or share your impressions—it's a fantastic way to foster connections.

Rennes' cultural experiences are not merely events; they are invitations to become an integral part of the city's living narrative. So, join the festivities, applaud the performances, and let Rennes' cultural richness unfold before you. The stage is set, and you are the protagonist in this captivating cultural journey. Enjoy the show!

Chapter 8: Dining

Prepare your taste buds for a culinary odyssey through the gastronomic delights of Rennes. From the rich tapestry of traditional Breton cuisine to the enchanting experiences offered by popular restaurants, dining in Rennes is a journey of flavors and a celebration of culinary artistry.

Traditional Cuisine

Feast on Tradition: Savoring Breton Culinary Treasures

1. **Galettes and Crêpes:**
Embark on a culinary adventure with the iconic Breton galettes and crêpes. Made from buckwheat flour, galettes are savory delights filled with an array of ingredients like cheese, ham, and eggs. For a sweet finale, indulge in a crêpe, delicately folded and brimming with tempting fillings such as Nutella, fruit compote, or caramel.

2. **Seafood Delicacies:**

As Rennes is situated in the Brittany region, seafood is a cornerstone of its cuisine. Dive into a platter of oysters, langoustines, or mussels, showcasing the freshness of the Atlantic. The coastal influence infuses these dishes with a briny essence that captivates the palate.

3. **Kouign-Amann**:

Indulge your sweet tooth with Kouign-Amann, a buttery Breton pastry that translates to "butter cake." Layers of dough and sugar are baked to perfection, creating a caramelized exterior that shatters with each bite. This delectable treat is a testament to the Breton commitment to craftsmanship in the kitchen.

4. **Cider**:

Complement your meal with a glass of Breton cider, a regional specialty. The effervescence of this apple-based beverage adds a refreshing note to your dining experience. Explore the diverse range of ciders, from sweet to dry, and discover the perfect pairing for your chosen dish.

Popular Restaurants

Haute Cuisine and Hidden Gems: Rennes' Culinary Hotspots

1. **La Cigale:**

Step into the grandeur of La Cigale, a historical brasserie that has been a Rennes institution since 1895. This iconic establishment offers a blend of Art Nouveau elegance and a menu featuring classic French dishes. From escargot to coq au vin, La Cigale invites you to savor the essence of French culinary tradition.

2. **Le Saint Georges:**

For a taste of modern Breton cuisine, venture to Le Saint Georges. This restaurant artfully combines local ingredients with contemporary flair, presenting dishes that are both innovative and rooted in tradition. Enjoy the sophisticated ambiance as you explore a menu that pays homage to the region's culinary heritage.

3. **Le Galopin:**

Nestled in the heart of Rennes, Le Galopin is a hidden gem known for its intimate setting and seasonal menu. The chef's dedication to fresh, local produce shines through in each dish. With a commitment to sustainability, Le Galopin offers a dining experience that harmonizes with the ethos of the Brittany region.

4. L'Écume des Mers:

Embark on a seafood journey at L'Écume des Mers, where the maritime spirit of Brittany takes center stage. The menu showcases an array of seafood delicacies, from platters of fruits de mer to exquisitely prepared fish dishes. Immerse yourself in a maritime-themed setting that echoes the coastal charm of Rennes' culinary scene.

Tips for Dining Etiquette

1. Reservations:

- Popular restaurants in Rennes often fill up quickly, especially during peak hours. To ensure a seamless dining experience, consider making reservations in advance. This ensures you secure a spot and allows the restaurant to cater to your preferences.

2. Opening Hours:

- Be mindful of the typical dining hours in Rennes. Lunch is generally served from around 12:00 PM to 2:00 PM, while dinner starts around 7:30 PM and may extend until 10:00 PM. Arriving during these hours ensures you have ample time to savor your meal without feeling rushed.

3. **Tipping Culture:**
   - Tipping in Rennes is customary but not as extensively as in some other countries. A service charge is often included in the bill. However, it is customary to round up the total or leave a small additional tip for exceptional service.

4. **Language**:
   - While many restaurants in Rennes cater to English-speaking guests, learning a few basic French phrases can enhance your dining experience. Locals appreciate the effort, and it adds a personal touch to your interactions.

In Rennes, dining is not merely sustenance; it's a journey into the heart of Breton culture. From the comforting allure of traditional dishes to the innovative creations of popular restaurants, every meal tells a story of culinary mastery. So, pull up a chair, savor each bite, and let the flavors of Rennes linger on your palate. Bon appétit!

Chapter 9: Nightlife

As the sun dips below the horizon, Rennes transforms into a city that pulses with energy and excitement. Join me on a journey through the nocturnal tapestry of this vibrant city, where the nightlife is a kaleidoscope of lively bars, cozy pubs, and diverse entertainment options.

Bars and Pubs

Cheers to the Night: Rennes' Intoxicating Bar Scene

1. Le Saint-Michel:
Let's kick off our nocturnal adventure at Le Saint-Michel, a beloved bar nestled in the heart of Rennes. This iconic venue, with its lively atmosphere, offers a broad selection of drinks, from craft beers to classic cocktails. Join the eclectic crowd, enjoy live music, and feel the pulse of Rennes' social heartbeat.

2. Melody Maker:

For music enthusiasts seeking a melodic escape, Melody Maker is a haven of rhythm and libations. This trendy bar, adorned with vintage album covers, invites you to savor creative cocktails while grooving to the beats of live bands or DJs. Immerse yourself in the harmonious vibes of Melody Maker.

3. **Comptoir du Roi Arthur:**

Step into the medieval-inspired ambiance of Comptoir du Roi Arthur, where history meets modern conviviality. This themed pub, complete with wooden beams and rustic decor, offers an extensive selection of beers, including local brews. Unwind in this cozy setting, surrounded by the warmth of camaraderie.

4. **Oan's Pub:**

Oan's Pub, with its Irish charm, adds an international flair to Rennes' nightlife. This welcoming pub, adorned with dark wood and Celtic motifs, serves up a variety of beers and spirits. Engage in lively conversations with locals and fellow travelers, creating memories as spirited as the ambiance.

Entertainment Options

A Night of Diverse Delights: Rennes' Entertaining Extravaganza

1. Le Liberté:
For a night of cultural enrichment, Le Liberté stands as Rennes' premier venue for concerts, theater performances, and artistic events. This contemporary space hosts a variety of shows, ranging from international music acts to thought-provoking plays. Check the schedule and elevate your night with a touch of cultural splendor.

2. L'Aire Libre:
Step into the realm of contemporary performing arts at L'Aire Libre, a cultural space that transcends conventional boundaries. This avant-garde venue showcases innovative dance performances, experimental theater, and interdisciplinary art installations. Immerse yourself in the cutting-edge creations that grace the stages of L'Aire Libre.

3. Le Panama Club:
Dance the night away at Le Panama Club, a pulsating venue that ignites the city's nightlife. This electrifying club hosts eclectic DJ sets, themed parties, and live performances. Lose yourself in the rhythm of the music, surrounded by the energetic vibes of Rennes' nocturnal revelry.

4. **Le 1929:**

If you're in the mood for a cinematic escape, Le 1929 offers a cozy setting for film enthusiasts. This independent cinema screens a curated selection of films, from arthouse gems to international releases. Grab some popcorn, settle into a comfortable seat, and let the magic of cinema unfold.

Nightlife Tips

1. **Opening Hours:**
   - Rennes' nightlife often starts late, with bars and pubs bustling from around 8:00 PM onwards. Clubs and entertainment venues typically come alive after 10:00 PM. Embrace the unhurried rhythm of the night and plan your nocturnal escapades accordingly.

2. **Dress Code:**
   - While Rennes is generally laid-back, some venues may have specific dress codes, especially clubs and upscale bars. It's advisable to check in advance and dress accordingly to ensure a smooth entry into your chosen nightlife hotspot.

3. Explore Different Neighborhoods:

- Rennes boasts diverse neighborhoods, each with its own nightlife charm. From the historic center with its classic pubs to the trendy districts with modern clubs, exploring different areas enhances your nocturnal adventure.

4. Be Open to Spontaneity:

- Some of the best experiences in Rennes' nightlife happen spontaneously. Strike up conversations with locals, follow the sounds of live music, or wander into a charming pub tucked away in a side street. Embrace the unpredictability of the night, and you might discover hidden gems.

Rennes' nightlife is a dynamic fusion of conviviality, entertainment, and cultural richness. So, as the stars emerge in the Breton sky, let the city's nocturnal offerings guide you through a night of merriment and memories. Cheers to the enchanting nightlife of Rennes!

Chapter 10: Shopping

Welcome to the shopper's haven in Rennes, where every cobblestone street and bustling market unveils a treasure trove of local delights. From the vibrant energy of local markets to the charming allure of unique boutiques, Rennes beckons you to explore its diverse shopping scene.

Local Markets

Market Marvels: Exploring Rennes' Lively Bazaars

1. **Marché des Lices:**
Our shopping odyssey begins at the iconic Marché des Lices, a vibrant market that has been a Rennes tradition since 1622. Every Saturday, locals and visitors alike gather to peruse the stalls brimming with fresh produce, regional delicacies, and artisanal crafts. From Breton cheeses to colorful flowers, this market is a sensory delight.

2. Marché du Mail:

For a taste of local flavor in a more intimate setting, Marché du Mail is a charming alternative. This market, held on Wednesday and Saturday mornings, showcases a delightful array of fruits, vegetables, and specialty foods. Stroll through the stalls, interact with friendly vendors, and savor the authentic atmosphere of this neighborhood market.

3. Marché Maurepas:

Discover the diverse cultural influences in Rennes at Marché Maurepas, where an array of global flavors converges. This market, held on Friday afternoons and evenings, features stalls offering spices, exotic fruits, and international cuisine. Immerse yourself in the vibrant tapestry of world cuisine right in the heart of Rennes.

4. Halles Centrales:

For an indoor market experience, Halles Centrales awaits with a plethora of gastronomic delights. Open throughout the week, this covered market houses a variety of stalls selling fresh seafood, meats, cheeses, and more. Let the aromas and colors guide you through a culinary journey within its bustling halls.

Unique Boutiques

Boutique Bliss: Rennes' Quirky and Chic Shopping Havens

1. **Rue Vasselot:**

Navigate the chic boutiques of Rue Vasselot, a street where fashion meets charm. This bustling avenue is adorned with an array of unique shops, from stylish clothing boutiques to artisanal craft stores. Explore the curated selections and discover one-of-a-kind fashion pieces that reflect Rennes' eclectic style.

2. **L'Éclaireur**:

For those with an eye for design and elegance, L'Éclaireur is a must-visit concept store. This boutique, situated in the heart of Rennes, features a carefully curated collection of fashion, accessories, and home decor. Each item exudes a sense of sophistication and artistic flair, making it a haven for discerning shoppers.

3. **Les Champs Libres Boutiques:**

Extend your shopping spree to Les Champs Libres, where a cluster of boutiques awaits within this cultural complex. These boutiques offer a diverse range of products, from literature and stationery to unique gifts and accessories.

Browse through the selections and bring home a piece of Rennes' cultural and artistic essence.

4. Ateliers Boutiques de la Vilaine:

Immerse yourself in the creativity of local artisans at Ateliers Boutiques de la Vilaine. This collective space gathers various workshops and boutiques, allowing you to explore handmade crafts, jewelry, and artistic creations. Support local artists and find distinctive souvenirs that capture the spirit of Rennes.

Shopping Tips

1. Cash and Cards:

- While larger establishments accept cards, it's advisable to carry some cash, especially when exploring local markets and smaller boutiques. Many vendors appreciate cash transactions, and it ensures a smoother shopping experience.

2. Local Artisans:

- Engage with local artisans and vendors. Whether it's striking up a conversation at a market stall or learning about the inspiration behind a handmade item in a boutique, connecting with the creators adds a personal touch to your shopping experience.

3. **Market Timing**:
- To fully experience the energy of local markets, consider visiting earlier in the day when stalls are freshly stocked, and the atmosphere is at its liveliest. This also provides the opportunity to interact with vendors and learn more about the products.

4. **Be Open to Discoveries:**
- Some of the most memorable finds come from unexpected places. Be open to exploring side streets, hidden alleys, and smaller boutiques. Rennes' charm lies not only in its main shopping areas but also in the surprises waiting to be uncovered off the beaten path.

Rennes' shopping landscape is a mosaic of traditional markets and eclectic boutiques, each offering a unique facet of the city's culture and craftsmanship. So, set forth on a shopping adventure, where every purchase becomes a cherished memory of your time in this enchanting Breton city. Happy shopping in Rennes!

Chapter 11: Day Trips

As we unfold the map of possibilities around Rennes, prepare to embark on enchanting day trips that reveal the diverse landscapes and rich cultural tapestry of Brittany. From ancient castles to coastal retreats, each nearby destination offers a unique adventure, just a short journey from the heart of Rennes.

Mont Saint-Michel

The Fairytale on the Horizon: A Day at Mont Saint-Michel

Approximately a 1.5-hour drive from Rennes, Mont Saint-Michel emerges like a mirage on the horizon. This UNESCO World Heritage site is a mesmerizing blend of medieval architecture and natural beauty. As you approach across the causeway, the abbey seems to float on the bay, surrounded by the ebb and flow of tides.

Highlights:

- *Abbey of Mont Saint-Michel:* Explore the abbey perched atop the rocky island, where narrow streets wind their way to stunning panoramic views.
- Medieval Streets: Wander through the charming medieval streets filled with shops, cafes, and historic houses.
- *Tidal Phenomenon:* Experience the unique tidal phenomenon, where the bay witnesses some of the most significant tides in Europe.

Mont Saint-Michel is a captivating day trip, transporting you to a world where history meets the ethereal beauty of the French coastline.

Saint-Malo

Walled Marvel by the Sea: Saint-Malo's Maritime Charms

Just over an hour's drive from Rennes lies the fortified city of Saint-Malo. This coastal gem, surrounded by sturdy ramparts, beckons with tales of corsairs and seafaring adventures.

Highlights:

- *Intra-Muros*: Explore the historic heart of Saint-Malo within the city walls, known as Intra-Muros, where narrow streets lead to bustling squares and sea views.
- *Fort National*: Visit Fort National, a fortress on a tidal island accessible during low tide, offering panoramic views of the city and coastline.
- *Grand Bé and Petit Bé Islands:* Take a boat to the nearby islands of Grand Bé and Petit Bé for scenic walks and a glimpse of the city from a different perspective.

Saint-Malo is a maritime haven, inviting you to stroll along its ramparts, breathe in the salty air, and immerse yourself in its seafaring ambiance.

Brocéliande Forest

Whispers of Legend: Mystical Day in Brocéliande Forest

Embark on a mystical journey into the heart of Brittany with a day trip to Brocéliande Forest, approximately a 45-minute drive from Rennes. Steeped in Arthurian legend, this enchanted forest captivates with its ancient trees, moss-covered stones, and magical ambiance.

Highlights:

- *Val sans Retour*: Discover Val sans Retour, a valley with the mythical "Valley of No Return," linked to the legend of Sir Lancelot and Queen Guinevere.
- *Merlin's Tomb:* Visit the "Tomb of Merlin" and the nearby Fontaine de Jouvence, believed to have magical properties.
- *Huelgoat*: Explore Huelgoat, a neighboring forest with massive boulders and the iconic "Chaos du Moulin," a landscape shaped by ancient geological forces.

Brocéliande Forest invites you to step into the realm of legends, where whispers of ancient tales linger among the ancient trees.

Dinan

Medieval Marvels: A Day in the Timeless Town of Dinan

A little over an hour's drive from Rennes, Dinan unfolds as a medieval masterpiece. This well-preserved town along the Rance River invites you to wander through cobbled streets and experience the charm of a bygone era.

Highlights:

- *Dinan Castle:* Explore Dinan Castle, perched on a hill, offering panoramic views of the town and surrounding countryside.
- *Rue du Jerzual:* Stroll along Rue du Jerzual, a picturesque street lined with half-timbered houses, boutiques, and cafes.
- *Dinan's Port:* Visit Dinan's port on the Rance River, where charming riverside cafes and boats bobbing on the water create a tranquil setting.

Dinan transports you back in time, allowing you to immerse yourself in medieval architecture and the ambiance of a historic Breton town.

Cancale

Seaside Serenity: Cancale's Coastal Charms

Less than an hour's drive from Rennes, Cancale awaits on the Emerald Coast. This quaint fishing village is renowned for its oysters and panoramic coastal views.

Highlights:

- *Oyster Farms*: Visit one of the oyster farms and enjoy fresh oysters with a view of the sea.
- *Pointe du Grouin*: Hike to Pointe du Grouin, a headland offering breathtaking views of the coastline and the nearby Mont Saint-Michel.
- *Port de la Houle:* Wander along the charming Port de la Houle, where fishing boats bob in the harbor and seafood restaurants beckon.

Cancale is a serene coastal escape, inviting you to savor the simplicity of seaside life and indulge in the region's renowned oysters.

Tips for Day Trips

1. **Plan Ahead:**
Check the opening hours and any special events at your chosen destination. Some attractions may have specific visiting times or seasonal variations.

2. **Transportation**:
Consider your preferred mode of transportation for day trips. Whether it's renting a car, joining guided tours, or using public transportation, choose the option that aligns with your preferences and schedule.

3. **Weather Considerations**:
Brittany's weather can vary, so pack accordingly. For coastal destinations, a light jacket and comfortable shoes are advisable. Check the weather forecast before heading out.

4. **Local Cuisine:**

Explore the culinary specialties of each destination. Whether it's sampling oysters in Cancale or savoring crepes in Saint-Malo, indulging in local cuisine enhances your day trip experience.

Day trips from Rennes offer a kaleidoscope of experiences, from medieval marvels to coastal serenity. As you venture beyond the city, let each destination paint a new chapter in your Breton adventure. Bon voyage on your day trips from Rennes!

Chapter 12: Outdoor Activities

Hiking and Nature

Nature's Canvas: Exploring Rennes' Hiking Trails and Natural Beauty

1. **Parc du Thabor**

Our journey into Rennes' outdoor wonders begins with Parc du Thabor, a botanical and floral park that seamlessly combines natural beauty with landscaped elegance. Located in the heart of the city, this expansive green oasis invites you to wander through lush gardens, breathe in the fragrance of blooming flowers, and unwind in serene surroundings.

Highlights:

- *Formal French Gardens*: Immerse yourself in the meticulously manicured formal French gardens, adorned with fountains and sculptures.

- *The Gloriette*: Discover the Gloriette, a charming pavilion nestled amidst vibrant flowerbeds, offering a peaceful retreat.
- *Woodland Trails:* Explore the woodland trails, where ancient trees provide shade, and the sounds of nature create a tranquil ambiance.

2. **Bois de L'Épinay**

For those seeking a more immersive natural experience, Bois de L'Épinay, a forested area just a short drive from Rennes, beckons with its extensive network of hiking trails. This enchanting forest allows you to reconnect with nature, offering a serene escape from the urban bustle.

Highlights:

- *Hiking Trails:* Choose from a variety of hiking trails, ranging from easy strolls to more challenging paths, catering to different fitness levels.
- *Picnic Areas*: Take advantage of designated picnic areas scattered throughout the forest, providing a perfect setting to enjoy a meal surrounded by nature.

- *Wildlife Observation*: Keep an eye out for the diverse wildlife that inhabits the forest, from songbirds to small mammals.

3. Lac de Trémelin

Venture a bit farther to Lac de Trémelin, a picturesque lake surrounded by woodlands and meadows. This outdoor haven offers not only hiking opportunities but also a range of water-based activities for those inclined to explore the lake.

Highlights:

- *Hiking Trails Around the Lake*: Embark on scenic hiking trails that circumnavigate the lake, providing breathtaking views of the water and its natural surroundings.
- *Water Activities:* Try your hand at water activities like paddleboarding or rowing, immersing yourself in the serene waters of Lac de Trémelin.
- *Family-Friendly Atmosphere:* The lake's shores are dotted with family-friendly spaces, making it an ideal destination for a day of outdoor enjoyment with loved ones.

4. **Rocher du Feu**

For a hiking adventure that combines nature with historical intrigue, head to Rocher du Feu, a rocky outcrop overlooking the Ille-et-Rance Canal. This site not only offers panoramic views but also tells tales of ancient rituals and the mysteries of the past.

Highlights:

- *Panoramic Views:* Reach the summit for panoramic views of the canal and the surrounding countryside, providing a perfect vantage point for photography enthusiasts.
- *Historical Significance*: Discover the historical significance of Rocher du Feu, believed to have been a site for prehistoric fire ceremonies, adding an extra layer of fascination to your hike.

Sports and Recreation

Active Pursuits: Rennes' Playgrounds for Sports and Recreation

1. **Parc des Gayeulles**

Parc des Gayeulles stands as Rennes' premier destination for a wide range of sports and recreational activities. This expansive park, spanning over 100 hectares, offers a dynamic space for both thrill-seekers and those seeking leisurely pursuits.

Highlights:

- *Adventure Park:* Challenge yourself at the adventure park, featuring treetop courses and zip lines for an exhilarating experience.
- *Swimming Pools:* Cool off in the park's swimming pools during the warmer months, providing a refreshing respite.
- *Sports Facilities:* Utilize the various sports facilities, including tennis courts, soccer fields, and basketball courts, catering to diverse sporting interests.

2. **Parc Oberthur**

For a more relaxed yet active ambiance, Parc Oberthur offers a delightful setting where recreational opportunities blend seamlessly with natural charm. This park is a haven for those looking to engage in sports or simply unwind amid green surroundings.

Highlights:

- *Petanque Courts:* Engage in a game of pétanque at the dedicated courts, where the rhythmic clack of metal balls on gravel creates a leisurely atmosphere.
- *Open Spaces for Yoga and Tai Chi:* Embrace the open spaces for yoga or tai chi, providing a serene environment for mindful movement.
- *Children's Playground*: Families can enjoy the children's playground, ensuring that Parc Oberthur caters to various age groups.

3. **Stade Rennais FC**

For enthusiasts of the beautiful game, a visit to Roazhon Park, home of Stade Rennais FC, promises an exciting immersion into the world of football. Whether catching a match or taking a guided tour of the stadium, this experience allows you to feel the pulse of Rennes' football culture.

Highlights:

- *Football Matches:* Attend a live football match and witness the fervor of Stade Rennais FC's passionate fan base.
- *Stadium Tours:* Explore behind the scenes with a guided stadium tour, offering insights into the club's history and a chance to tread the hallowed turf.

4. **Golf de la Freslonnière**

For those seeking a more leisurely yet refined sporting experience, Golf de la Freslonnière presents an idyllic golfing retreat. Located in a picturesque countryside setting, this golf course provides a serene escape for golf enthusiasts.

Highlights:

- *18-Hole Course:* Enjoy a round of golf on the 18-hole course, where well-manicured fairways and challenging greens cater to golfers of all skill levels.
- *Scenic Views*: Revel in the scenic views of the surrounding countryside, creating a tranquil backdrop for a day on the golf course.
- *Golf Academy*: Improve your swing and technique with the guidance of the golf academy, making this destination welcoming for both beginners and seasoned players.

Tips for Outdoor Activities

1. **Weather Preparedness**:
   - Check the weather forecast before engaging in outdoor activities. Dress appropriately and carry essentials like sunscreen, water, and comfortable footwear.

2. **Trail Etiquette:**
   - When hiking, adhere to trail etiquette by staying on designated paths, respecting wildlife, and leaving no trace. This ensures a positive experience for both you and future visitors.

3. **Equipment Rental:**
   - For sports and recreational activities, consider equipment rental options available at certain parks or facilities. This is especially useful for activities like paddleboarding, zip-lining, or golfing.

4. **Local Events:**
   - Check for local events or sports matches taking place during your visit. Attending a local game or sports

event can add a cultural touch to your outdoor experience.

Whether you're drawn to the tranquility of nature hikes or the excitement of sports and recreation, Rennes offers a diverse array of outdoor activities. So, lace up your hiking boots, pack your sports gear, and embrace the outdoor playgrounds awaiting you in this captivating Breton city. Enjoy the fresh air and the beauty of Rennes' outdoor wonders!

Chapter 13:
Family-Friendly Rennes

Kid-Friendly Activities

Journeys of Wonder: Unveiling Rennes' Kid-Friendly Delights

1. Les Machines de l'île

Our adventure into family-friendly Rennes commences with Les Machines de l'île, a whimsical world where imagination takes flight. Inspired by the works of Jules Verne and Leonardo da Vinci, this captivating attraction brings mechanical marvels to life, offering a blend of artistry and play.

Highlights:

- *The Grand Elephant*: Marvel at The Grand Elephant, a colossal mechanical elephant that roams the grounds, inviting passengers for a magical ride.
- *Carousel of the Marine Worlds*: Experience the Carousel of the Marine Worlds, featuring fantastical sea creatures that spin and twirl, creating an enchanting spectacle.
- *Underwater World:* Explore the Underwater World, where mechanical sea creatures swim in a mesmerizing aquatic display.

2. **Planetarium de Bretagne**

For young stargazers and aspiring astronomers, the Planetarium de Bretagne awaits with celestial wonders and cosmic adventures. Situated within the Champs Libres cultural complex, this immersive experience offers a journey through the cosmos.

Highlights:

- *360-Degree Dome*: Enter the 360-degree dome of the planetarium, where stunning visuals transport you to distant galaxies and planets.

- *Educational Shows:* Enjoy educational shows tailored for different age groups, making astronomy accessible and engaging for children.
- *Interactive Exhibits:* Explore interactive exhibits that allow hands-on exploration of astronomical concepts, fostering curiosity and learning.

3. **Parc du Baud**

Parc du Baud, nestled in the heart of Rennes, unfolds as a haven for families seeking outdoor adventures and recreational delights. This expansive park offers a blend of green spaces, playgrounds, and activities suitable for children of all ages.

Highlights:

- *Adventure Playground*: Unleash the spirit of adventure at the park's expansive adventure playground, featuring climbing structures, slides, and creative play areas.
- *Miniature Train Rides:* Delight in miniature train rides that meander through the park, providing a charming tour of its scenic landscapes.

- *Duck Pond:* Visit the duck pond, where families can enjoy leisurely walks, feed the ducks, and bask in the tranquil ambiance of the park.

4. **Le Ludik Parc**

Le Ludik Parc emerges as a vibrant oasis of fun, designed to cater specifically to families with children. This indoor play space offers a dynamic environment where kids can explore, play, and let their imaginations run wild.

Highlights:

- *Play Zones*: Navigate through diverse play zones, including ball pits, climbing structures, and interactive games, ensuring a variety of activities for children of different ages.
- *Birthday Party Packages*: Le Ludik Parc also offers birthday party packages, allowing families to celebrate special occasions in a playful and festive setting.

Parks and Playgrounds

Green Havens: Rennes' Parks and Playgrounds for Family Bonding

1. **Parc des Gayeulles**

Our exploration of family-friendly parks and playgrounds begins with the expansive Parc des Gayeulles. This lush green space, spanning over 100 hectares, unfolds as a recreational haven for families seeking a blend of outdoor activities and natural beauty.

Highlights:

- *Play Areas for All Ages:* Discover play areas designed for different age groups, ensuring that toddlers and older children alike find engaging and age-appropriate activities.
- *Mini Golf:* Engage in a friendly game of mini-golf within the park, offering a leisurely yet entertaining experience for the whole family.
- *Boating Lake*: Enjoy the boating lake, where families can paddle together in small boats, creating moments of shared adventure.

2. **Parc Oberthur**

For families desiring a more relaxed and intimate park experience, Parc Oberthur presents itself as an inviting oasis. This charming green space, dotted with floral displays and open lawns, provides a tranquil setting for family picnics and leisurely strolls.

Highlights:

- *Botanical Gardens:* Explore the park's botanical gardens, where a diverse collection of plants and flowers adds a touch of natural splendor.
- *Children's Playground*: Let the little ones unleash their energy at the children's playground, equipped with swings, slides, and play structures.
- *Amphitheater*: Discover the amphitheater within the park, occasionally hosting cultural events and performances, adding an artistic touch to your visit.

3. **Parc du Thabor**

Parc du Thabor, a jewel in the heart of Rennes, unfolds as a picturesque setting where families can enjoy the beauty of landscaped gardens, play areas, and serene walking paths.

Highlights:

- *Rose Garden*: Stroll through the rose garden, where vibrant blooms create a fragrant and visually stunning backdrop.
- *Animal Statues:* Encounter whimsical animal statues scattered throughout the park, adding a playful element to your exploration.
- *Children's Play Zone:* Visit the dedicated children's play zone, featuring swings, climbing frames, and ample space for kids to engage in active play.

4. **Parc de Maurepas**

Parc de Maurepas, situated in the western part of Rennes, beckons families with its blend of natural landscapes, recreational facilities, and a welcoming atmosphere.

Highlights:

- *Wooden Play Structures:* Engage in imaginative play with the wooden play structures nestled within the park, fostering creativity and physical activity.
- *Fitness Trail:* For families seeking a bit of outdoor exercise, the fitness trail offers a well-designed circuit with exercise stations suitable for various fitness levels.

- *Open Spaces for Picnics:* Take advantage of the park's open spaces, ideal for family picnics, where you can savor a meal surrounded by nature.

Tips for Family-Friendly Exploration

1. Check Opening Hours:
Verify the opening hours of attractions, parks, and play areas. Some venues may have specific hours of operation, especially during weekends or holidays.

2. Weather-Appropriate Attire:
Dress the family in weather-appropriate attire, considering the day's forecast and the activities planned. Comfortable shoes for outdoor exploration are a must.

3. Snacks and Hydration:
Bring along snacks and sufficient water, especially when exploring parks and outdoor spaces. Having refreshments on hand ensures that energy levels remain high throughout the day.

4. plan age-appropriate activities:
Consider the age range of your children when planning activities. Rennes offers a diverse range of attractions

catering to various age groups, ensuring an inclusive and enjoyable experience for all family members.

Family-friendly Rennes welcomes you to a world of enchantment, where laughter echoes through parks, playgrounds spark creativity, and shared moments become cherished memories. So, gather your loved ones and embark on a journey of joy and discovery in this captivating Breton city. Happy exploring!

Chapter 14: Local Events

The Rhythms of Rennes: A Calendar of Vibrant Local Events

The Heartbeat of Rennes

As you delve into the local tapestry of Rennes, you'll discover a city pulsating with life, where each month unfolds with a symphony of events that resonate with the spirit of the Breton people. From cultural festivals to lively markets, Rennes' calendar of events is a kaleidoscope of experiences that immerses you in the heart and soul of this vibrant city.

January

Trans Musicales

Kickstarting the year with a burst of musical energy, Trans Musicales takes center stage in January. This internationally acclaimed music festival showcases emerging artists and diverse genres, turning Rennes into a melting pot of musical innovation. From indie bands to electronic beats, Trans

Musicales is a celebration of the avant-garde, inviting you to witness the next wave of musical talent.

February

Les Embellies Festival

As winter begins to wane, Les Embellies Festival emerges to infuse the city with artistic flair. This independent music festival celebrates creativity and diversity, featuring a lineup of indie, folk, and alternative acts. Attend intimate performances in unique venues across Rennes, where the city itself becomes a canvas for musical expression.

March

Mythos Festival

March unfolds with the Mythos Festival, a captivating celebration of storytelling in all its forms. From literature to theater, this festival weaves tales that captivate audiences of all ages. Explore the enchanting streets of Rennes as they come alive with performances, workshops, and storytelling events that transport you to realms of imagination.

April

Saint George's Day Market

As spring blooms, Rennes hosts the Saint George's Day Market, a delightful showcase of local artisans and craftsmen. Stroll through the cobblestone streets, where stalls brim with handmade treasures, artisanal foods, and vibrant flowers. The market's festive atmosphere invites you to indulge in the best of Breton craftsmanship.

May

Rennes International Jazz Festival

May brings the Rennes International Jazz Festival, a harmonious celebration that echoes through the city's squares and venues. Immerse yourself in the soulful notes of jazz as both local and international artists grace the stage. From smooth melodies to lively improvisations, the festival transforms Rennes into a haven for jazz enthusiasts.

June

Les Tombées de la Nuit

As summer approaches, Les Tombées de la Nuit takes Rennes by storm. This multidisciplinary arts festival brings the streets to life with theatrical performances, dance, and visual arts. Join the lively crowds as the city becomes a stage for creativity, offering a magical blend of entertainment and cultural exploration.

July

Rennes sur Roulettes
July rolls in with the exhilarating Rennes sur Roulettes, a rollerblading festival that adds a dash of adrenaline to the summer air. Watch as skilled skaters take to the streets in impressive displays, or join in the fun with family-friendly activities. Rennes sur Roulettes transforms the city into a dynamic playground on wheels.

August

La Route du Rock
August ushers in the renowned La Route du Rock, a music festival that has become a fixture in Rennes' cultural landscape. Set against the stunning backdrop of Fort Saint-Père, this indie and alternative music festival draws crowds from far and wide. Lose yourself in the eclectic sounds of La Route du Rock amid the historic ambiance of the fort.

September

Les Transats du Thabor

As the summer sun lingers, Les Transats du Thabor offers a serene respite in Parc du Thabor. This outdoor cinema event invites you to recline on deck chairs and enjoy film screenings beneath the stars. A perfect blend of relaxation and cinematic delight, Les Transats du Thabor brings a touch of magic to September evenings.

October

Yaouank Festival

October brings the Yaouank Festival, a celebration of Breton culture and traditional music. Dance to the lively tunes of Celtic melodies and witness the spectacle of Breton folk dances. Yaouank Festival captures the essence of Brittany's rich heritage, inviting you to participate in the joyous festivities.

November

Travelling Film Festival

November unfolds with the Travelling Film Festival, a cinematic journey that spans the globe. Explore diverse cultures through carefully curated films showcased in various venues across Rennes. Whether you're a film enthusiast or simply curious, the Travelling Film Festival offers a captivating cinematic experience.

December

Rennes Christmas Market

As the year draws to a close, Rennes transforms into a winter wonderland with the enchanting Christmas Market. Adorned with festive lights and the aroma of seasonal treats, the market invites you to explore stalls filled with handcrafted gifts, local delicacies, and holiday cheer. Embrace the warmth of the season as the city sparkles with festive spirit.

Tips for Navigating Local Events

1. **Plan Ahead:**
   - Check the event calendar in advance to align your visit with the festivals and activities that pique your interest.

2. **Local Insights:**

- Engage with locals to gather insights into the must-see events and hidden gems that might not be on the official calendar.

3. Cultural Immersion:
- Immerse yourself in the local culture by participating in traditional events and festivals, gaining a deeper understanding of Rennes' vibrant community.

4. Flexibility:
- While planning is key, be open to spontaneous discoveries. Rennes' dynamic atmosphere often unveils unexpected treasures during your explorations.

Embark on a journey through the annual rhythms of Rennes, where each month offers a unique melody of festivals, markets, and cultural experiences. Whether you're drawn to the beats of a music festival or the enchantment of a Christmas market, Rennes' calendar of events ensures that every visit becomes a celebration of life in this captivating Breton city. Enjoy the vibrant tapestry of Rennes' local events!

Chapter 15: Language and Local Etiquette

Unlocking the Heart of Rennes: Navigating Language and Embracing Cultural Etiquette

Useful Phrases

Basic Greetings:

Hello:

- French: Bonjour
- Pronunciation: Bon-zhoor

Goodbye:

- French: Au revoir
- Pronunciation: Oh ruh-vwar

Please:

- French: S'il vous plaît
- Pronunciation: Seel voo pleh

Thanks you:

- French: Merci
- Pronunciation: Mehr-see

Excuse me / I'm sorry:

- French: Excusez-moi
- Pronunciation: Ex-kew-zay mwah

Yes:

- French: Oui
- Pronunciation: Wee

No:

- French: Non
- Pronunciation: Noh

Asking for Directions:

Where is...?:

- French: Où est...?
- Pronunciation: Oo eh...?

How do I get to...?:

- French: Comment aller à...?
- Pronunciation: Koh-mohn ah-lay ah...?

Is it far?:

- French: C'est loin?
- Pronunciation: Say lwah?

Can you help me?:

- French: Pouvez-vous m'aider?
- Pronunciation: Poo-veh voo meh-dey?

Ordering Food:

Menu, please:

- French: La carte, s'il vous plaît
- Pronunciation: Lah kart, seel voo pleh

I would like...:

- French: Je voudrais...
- Pronunciation: Zhuh voo-dray...

Water:

- French: Eau
- Pronunciation: Oh

Check, please:

- French: L'addition, s'il vous plaît
- Pronunciation: Lah-dee-syon, seel voo pleh

<u>**Emergencies:**</u>

Help!:

- French: Au secours!
- Pronunciation: Oh suh-koor!

I need a doctor:

- French: J'ai besoin d'un médecin
- Pronunciation: Zhay buh-zwah duhn may-deh-sahn

Where is the hospital?:

- French: Où est l'hôpital?
- Pronunciation: Oo eh loh-pee-tahl?

Cultural Norms

Greetings and Politeness:

La Bise:

- In France, it's common to greet friends and acquaintances with a kiss on both cheeks, known as "la bise." The number of kisses varies by region, so follow the lead of locals.

Formal vs. Informal:

- Address strangers, elders, or those in professional settings with formal expressions (using "vous"), while informal expressions (using "tu") are reserved for friends and family.

Dining Etiquette:

Dining Pace:

- Meals in France are savored and often take longer than in some other cultures. Take your time, enjoy the conversation, and relish each course.

Bread Etiquette:

- Break a piece of bread, don't cut it with a knife. It's a customary gesture that signifies camaraderie and sharing.

Wine Tasting:

- When presented with wine, hold the glass by the stem to avoid warming the wine. A simple "Santé!" (Cheers) before taking a sip is appreciated.

Public Spaces:

Quiet Public Transport:

- Conversations on public transportation are generally kept at a low volume, respecting the quiet atmosphere.

Respect Personal Space:

- Personal space is valued in France. Maintain a reasonable distance when conversing and avoid unnecessary physical contact.

Shopping Etiquette:

Greetings in Shops:

- Greet shopkeepers with a polite "Bonjour" upon entering, and "Au revoir" when leaving.

Bagging Groceries:

- In supermarkets, you'll often need to bag your own groceries. Be prepared to do so after paying.

Festivals and Events:

Respecting Traditions:

- During festivals and cultural events, respect local traditions and participate with an open mind. This may include costume parades, traditional music, or dances.

Photography Etiquette:

- Ask for permission before taking photos of individuals, especially during festivals or in more private settings.

<u>Language Etiquette:</u>

Learn Basic French Phrases:

- While many locals in Rennes speak English, making an effort to learn a few basic French phrases is appreciated and can enhance your experience.

Patience in Communication:

- French communication tends to be more direct and formal. Be patient and listen actively, even if the conversation seems brisk.

<u>General Tips:</u>

Tipping Practices:

- Tipping is included in service charges at restaurants, but it's common to leave small change. In cafes, rounding up is customary.

Be Punctual:

- Punctuality is valued in France. If invited to someone's home, arriving a little early is polite.

Dress Modestly:

- While Rennes is modern, dressing modestly is appreciated, especially when visiting religious sites or attending formal events.

Quiet Sundays:

- Sundays are often quieter, with some businesses closed. Plan accordingly and enjoy a leisurely day exploring parks or cultural sites.

Embracing the local language and cultural norms in Rennes opens doors to meaningful connections and a richer travel experience. So, practice your "bonjours," savor the nuances of "la bise," and let the heart of Rennes reveal itself through its language and etiquette. Bon voyage!

Chapter 16: Safety Tips

Your Guardian Companion: Navigating Rennes with Safety in Mind

Emergency Contacts

Medical Emergencies:

Emergency Services:
In case of immediate medical assistance, dial 112. This connects you to emergency services, including ambulances and paramedics.

Hospitals:
If you need to locate the nearest hospital, Centre Hospitalier Universitaire de Rennes (CHU Rennes) is a major medical center in the city.

- *Address*: 2 Rue Henri Le Guilloux, 35033 Rennes, France

- *Emergency Department*: +33 2 99 28 43 21

Pharmacies:

For non-emergency medical needs or medication, local pharmacies ("pharmacie" in French) can assist. They usually have a rotating schedule for after-hours service.

Police Assistance:

Police Emergency:

For immediate police assistance, dial 17. This connects you to the national emergency police line.

Police Station - Rennes Centre:

If you need to visit a police station, the central police station in Rennes is easily accessible.
- *Address*: 3 Rue Martenot, 35000 Rennes, France
- *Non-emergency line*: +33 2 99 79 79 79

Consular Services:

Embassy Contacts:

For consular assistance from your home country, contact your embassy or consulate. If you're unsure of the contact details, most embassies have a 24/7 emergency hotline.

General Safety Guidelines

Public Transportation Safety:

Keep Valuables Secure:
While using public transportation, keep your belongings secure. Be mindful of your bags and pockets to prevent pickpocketing.

Follow Timetables:
Stay informed about public transportation schedules. Plan your journeys to avoid being stranded, especially during late hours.

Street Safety:

Well-lit Areas:
Stick to well-lit and populated areas, especially during the night. Avoid poorly lit or isolated streets.

Cross Streets Safely:
Use designated crosswalks when crossing streets. Obey traffic signals, and be cautious of cyclists and pedestrians.

Personal Safety:

Awareness is Key:
Stay aware of your surroundings. Be mindful of who is around you, especially in crowded areas or public transportation.

Emergency Apps:
Consider downloading local emergency apps that provide real-time information and alerts. These can be valuable tools during unforeseen situations.

Health and Hygiene:

Health Precautions:
Carry basic health supplies, such as hand sanitizer and tissues. Ensure you have any necessary medications and a small first aid kit.

Safe Food Practices:
Enjoy the local cuisine but be cautious about food safety. Choose reputable eateries, and drink bottled water if unsure of tap water quality.

Cultural Sensitivity:

Respect Local Customs:
Familiarize yourself with local customs and cultural norms. Respectful behavior enhances your safety and enriches your cultural experience.

Language Assistance:
Learn basic local phrases for assistance. Locals appreciate the effort, and it can be helpful in communication, especially in emergencies.

Weather Preparedness:

Check Weather Forecasts:
Stay updated on weather forecasts. Rennes experiences a temperate oceanic climate, so it's advisable to be prepared for occasional rain.

Sun Protection:
If visiting during sunny seasons, use sunscreen, wear a hat, and stay hydrated to protect yourself from the sun.

Digital Safety:

Secure Personal Devices:

Be cautious with personal devices. Keep them secure and avoid displaying valuables in public.

Use Reputable Wi-Fi:

When using public Wi-Fi, choose reputable networks to protect your data. Consider using a Virtual Private Network (VPN) for added security.

Transportation Safety:

Use Licensed Taxis:

When using taxis, ensure they are licensed. Verify with your accommodation or local authorities for reputable taxi services.

Driving Safety:

If driving, adhere to local traffic rules. Familiarize yourself with road signs and be cautious, especially in unfamiliar areas.

Tips for a Safe and Enjoyable Stay

1. Emergency Information:

- Save emergency contacts on your phone and have a physical copy in case of device failure.

2. Share Your Plans:
- Inform someone trustworthy about your daily plans, especially if you're exploring alone.

3. Travel Insurance:
- Consider travel insurance that covers medical emergencies, trip cancellations, and other unforeseen events.

4. Know Your Embassy:
- Be aware of your embassy's location and contact details. They can assist in emergencies and provide consular services.

5. Trust Your Instincts:
- If something feels off, trust your instincts. Avoid situations or places that make you uncomfortable.

6. Stay Informed:
- Keep yourself informed about local news and any potential travel advisories.

7. **Cultural Awareness:**
- Embrace the local culture while being mindful of cultural differences. This enhances your safety and overall experience.

Safety is paramount as you explore the enchanting streets of Rennes. By following these guidelines and staying vigilant, you can ensure a secure and enjoyable journey through this captivating Breton city. Bon voyage and stay safe!

Chapter 17: Sustainability in Rennes

Harmony with Nature: Navigating Eco-Friendly Rennes

Eco-Friendly Practices

1. **Public Transportation Prowess:**
Rennes takes a green leap with its efficient and eco-friendly public transportation system. Opt for buses or the metro, which are not only convenient but also contribute to reducing carbon emissions. The city is designed to encourage cycling and walking, promoting a healthier and more sustainable way to explore.

2. **Biking Bliss:**
Rennes is a cyclist's haven, with dedicated bike lanes weaving through the city. Embrace sustainable travel by renting a bike from various providers. Pedal your way through the

charming streets, discovering hidden gems and contributing to the city's commitment to eco-friendly mobility.

3. **Waste Not, Want Not:**
Waste management in Rennes is a model of sustainability. The city encourages recycling, and you'll find separate bins for different types of waste. Be a responsible traveler by disposing of your waste thoughtfully, contributing to Rennes' efforts to maintain its eco-friendly ethos.

4. **Green Spaces Galore:**
Rennes proudly boasts numerous green spaces, providing a breath of fresh air in the urban landscape. Parc du Thabor, Parc des Gayeulles, and Parc Oberthur are just a few examples. These oases not only enhance the city's aesthetics but also act as vital lungs, promoting biodiversity and offering residents and visitors alike a serene escape.

5. **Farmers' Market Finesse:**
Dive into Rennes' culinary scene while supporting sustainable practices by exploring the vibrant farmers' markets. Marché des Lices, one of the largest markets in France, offers a cornucopia of fresh, local produce. Engage with farmers, learn about sustainable agriculture, and savor the flavors of responsibly sourced ingredients.

Responsible Tourism

6. Cultural Respect:

Immerse yourself in the local culture with a respectful attitude. Engage with the community, learn about traditions, and be mindful of cultural nuances. Responsible tourism involves leaving a positive impact, fostering understanding and appreciation for the destination.

7. Support Local:

Rennes is a city that treasures its local businesses. From quaint boutiques to family-run eateries, supporting local establishments contributes to the economic sustainability of the community. Indulge in authentic experiences, and your travel footprint becomes a positive one.

8. Eco-Conscious Accommodations:

Choose accommodations that prioritize sustainability. Many hotels and guesthouses in Rennes are adopting eco-friendly practices, such as energy-efficient lighting, waste reduction initiatives, and water-saving measures. By opting for such stays, you actively participate in responsible tourism.

9. Eclectic Eco-Events:

Keep an eye out for eco-conscious events during your visit. Rennes hosts various sustainability-focused gatherings, workshops, and markets. These events not only provide valuable insights into green practices but also offer opportunities to engage with like-minded individuals and local eco-activists.

10. Nature-Friendly Exploration:

Rennes' surrounding areas are adorned with natural wonders. When venturing into nature, follow established trails, respect wildlife, and leave no trace. Responsible exploration ensures the preservation of the breathtaking landscapes that make Rennes and its vicinity so enchanting.

11. Culinary Conscientiousness:

Rennes' culinary scene embraces sustainability, with many restaurants adopting farm-to-table practices. Enjoy meals made from locally sourced ingredients, supporting regional farmers and reducing the carbon footprint associated with food transportation.

12. Educate and Advocate:

Be an ambassador for sustainable practices. Share your eco-friendly experiences in Rennes through social media or travel platforms. Your advocacy can inspire others to adopt responsible tourism habits, creating a ripple effect for positive change.

13. Water Wisdom:

Conserve water during your stay by practicing mindful usage. Whether in your accommodation or public spaces, adopting water-saving habits aligns with Rennes' commitment to environmental responsibility.

14. Mindful Mobility:

Explore Rennes by foot or public transport whenever possible. By minimizing the use of private vehicles, you contribute to reducing air pollution and easing traffic congestion, aligning with the city's vision for sustainable urban mobility.

15. Seasonal Sensibility:

Plan your visit with an awareness of the seasons. Certain times of the year may offer specific eco-friendly activities or events, such as environmental awareness campaigns or community clean-up initiatives.

Rennes' Path to Sustainability

Rennes is on a steadfast journey towards a sustainable future. From innovative urban planning to community-driven initiatives, the city is weaving environmental consciousness into its very fabric. As you explore the charming streets and embrace the warmth of Breton hospitality, remember that your choices can contribute to the city's eco-friendly evolution.

Top Tips for Responsible Travel in Rennes:

1. **Eco-Friendly Transit:**
   - Opt for public transportation, walking, or cycling to minimize your carbon footprint.

2. **Support Local Businesses**:
   - Choose local eateries, shops, and accommodations that prioritize sustainability.

3. **Reduce, Reuse, Recycle:**
   - Follow waste management guidelines and actively participate in recycling efforts.

4. **Cultural Respect:**
   - Engage with locals respectfully, appreciating and learning from their cultural practices.

5. **Nature Preservation:**
- Contribute to the preservation of natural spaces by practicing responsible exploration.

6. **Spread Awareness:**
- Share your sustainable travel experiences to inspire others and promote responsible tourism.

In every step you take and every choice you make, let your journey through Rennes be a testament to the beauty of responsible travel. Embrace the city's eco-friendly spirit, and may your exploration be a harmonious dance with nature and culture. Bon voyage on your sustainable sojourn in Rennes!

Chapter 18: Technology and Connectivity

Stay Connected in Style: Navigating the Tech Landscape in Rennes

Internet Access

1. **Citywide Wi-Fi Wonder**:
Rennes is a city that embraces the digital age with open arms. Enjoy seamless internet access in various public spaces, thanks to the city's extensive Wi-Fi network. From charming cafes to bustling squares, stay connected effortlessly while soaking in the Breton atmosphere.

2. **Café Culture and Connectivity:**
Dive into Rennes' renowned café culture while staying connected. Many cafes offer free Wi-Fi to patrons. Sip on a cup of locally brewed coffee or indulge in a delectable pastry

while catching up on emails or sharing your latest adventure on social media.

3. **Libraries for Tech Enthusiasts:**
If you prefer a tranquil setting for work or study, Rennes' libraries are havens of connectivity. Libraries such as Bibliothèque des Champs Libres provide not only a peaceful environment but also free Wi-Fi access, allowing you to blend work and exploration seamlessly.

4. **Co-Working Spaces:**
For digital nomads or those seeking a dedicated workspace, Rennes offers co-working spaces equipped with high-speed internet. Connect with like-minded individuals, tap into the city's vibrant professional scene, and make the most of modern amenities tailored for remote work.

5. **Accommodations Amped with Connectivity:**
Hotels and guesthouses in Rennes understand the importance of connectivity for modern travelers. Enjoy complimentary Wi-Fi in your accommodation, ensuring you can plan your adventures, stay in touch with loved ones, or simply unwind with your favorite digital content.

6. **Tech Stores for Quick Fixes**:

In the unlikely event of any tech hiccups, Rennes has tech stores and service centers. Whether you need a quick fix or a replacement, these stores cater to various tech needs, ensuring your devices stay in top shape throughout your visit.

Mobile Services

7. **Local SIM Card Convenience**:

Enhance your connectivity with a local SIM card. Purchase one from various providers easily accessible in the city. This allows you to enjoy affordable data plans, local calls, and the flexibility to stay connected on the go.

8. **Major Mobile Operators:**

Rennes is well-served by major mobile operators such as Orange, SFR, and Bouygues Telecom. Their extensive coverage ensures you can explore the city and its surroundings without worrying about signal drop-offs.

9. **Prepaid vs. Postpaid Options**:

Choose between prepaid and postpaid mobile plans based on your preferences and the duration of your stay. Prepaid plans offer flexibility without long-term commitments, while postpaid plans might be suitable for longer visits.

10. **Top-Up and Recharge Ease:**
Topping up your mobile credit is a breeze in Rennes. Numerous convenience stores, kiosks, and online platforms offer easy ways to recharge your phone, ensuring you stay connected without interruption.

11. **Mobile Data Packages:**
Opt for mobile data packages that align with your usage patterns. Whether you're a social media enthusiast or a traveler who prefers navigation apps, choose a plan that caters to your specific needs.

12. **Public Transportation Apps:**
Make the most of Rennes' efficient public transportation with dedicated apps. Stay updated on schedules, plan routes, and navigate the city effortlessly with these user-friendly applications, adding a tech-savvy touch to your travel experience.

13. **Emergency Services Access:**
Save local emergency numbers and services on your phone for quick access. In case of any unforeseen circumstances,

having these contacts readily available ensures a prompt response when needed.

14. **Multilingual Assistance Apps:**

Language barriers need not be a concern in Rennes. Utilize translation apps that offer multilingual support. These tools can be invaluable when seeking information, communicating with locals, or simply immersing yourself in the rich cultural tapestry of the city.

Tech Tips for a Connected Journey

1. **Citywide Hotspots Map:**

Familiarize yourself with citywide Wi-Fi hotspots. Several maps and online resources provide insights into areas with free public Wi-Fi, making it easy to plan your connectivity during your explorations.

2. **Local SIM Registration:**

Ensure your local SIM card is registered as required by French regulations. Most providers offer straightforward registration processes, but it's a step worth considering for hassle-free usage.

3. **Offline Maps for Navigation:**

While Rennes is navigable with online maps, having offline maps downloaded can be handy, especially in areas with limited connectivity. Plan your routes in advance and explore with confidence.

4. Tech Support Contacts:

Save the contact details of tech support services or your device manufacturer's customer service in case you encounter any technical issues during your stay.

5. Adapters and Chargers:

Check the compatibility of your chargers and electronic devices with local power outlets. Carrying a universal adapter ensures you can charge your devices without any compatibility issues.

6. Secure Connectivity:

When using public Wi-Fi, especially for sensitive activities like online banking, consider using a Virtual Private Network (VPN) for added security.

7. Weather-Resistant Devices:

Be mindful of the weather, especially during rainy seasons. Investing in weather-resistant phone cases or covers ensures your devices stay protected from unexpected downpours.

8. **Explore Tech Events:**

Check for any tech-related events or conferences taking place in Rennes during your visit. These gatherings can provide unique insights into local tech innovations and offer networking opportunities.

Rennes seamlessly combines its rich cultural heritage with modern technological conveniences. Stay connected, capture every moment, and let technology enhance your journey through the enchanting streets and landscapes of this Breton gem. May your devices be charged, your connections strong, and your exploration of Rennes digitally delightful. Happy travels!

Chapter 19: Travel Tips from Locals

Unveiling Rennes' Hidden Treasures: Insights from the Heart of Breton Hospitality

Insider Recommendations

1. Embrace the Rhythm of Breton Time:
In Rennes, time seems to flow at its own unhurried pace. Locals cherish the art of savoring moments, whether at a café, in a park, or while strolling through the cobbled streets. Embrace this relaxed rhythm, allowing yourself the pleasure of truly experiencing the city.

2. Navigate Like a Local:
Rennes is a city designed for exploration by foot or bicycle. Follow the lead of locals and wander through the historic center's winding alleys, discovering tucked-away boutiques,

cozy bistros, and vibrant street art. It's the best way to absorb the authentic charm of the city.

3. **Savor the Café Culture**:

Bretons have perfected the art of café culture, and Rennes is no exception. Engage in the local pastime of people-watching while sipping on a coffee at a bustling café. Whether you choose a terrace in Place des Lices or a cozy spot in Saint-Anne, immerse yourself in the café ambiance.

4. **Market Magic at Marché des Lices:**

Saturdays come alive at Marché des Lices, one of the largest markets in France. Locals frequent this bustling marketplace to shop for fresh produce, cheeses, and regional specialties. Join the vibrant atmosphere, sample local delights, and engage with vendors for an authentic Breton market experience.

5. **Festive Fridays at Place Sainte-Anne:**

Fridays bring a lively energy to Place Sainte-Anne. Join the locals at the many bars and restaurants surrounding the square. It's the perfect spot to unwind, enjoy live music, and soak in the convivial atmosphere that characterizes Rennes' nightlife.

6. Picnic in Parc du Thabor:

Parc du Thabor is a beloved oasis in the heart of Rennes. Follow the lead of locals and pack a picnic. Find a shaded spot under the trees, by the ornate fountain, or near the charming rose garden. It's a favorite pastime for families, friends, and couples alike.

7. Discover the Street Art Scene:

Rennes is a canvas of vibrant street art. Locals often take pride in the city's ever-evolving murals and installations. Wander through neighborhoods like La Courrouze and Maurepas to discover hidden artistic gems and witness the dynamic expression of Breton creativity.

8. Explore Beyond the Historic Center:

While the historic center is enchanting, locals recommend venturing beyond. Explore the lesser-known neighborhoods, like Cleunay or Francisco Ferrer, to discover a more authentic side of Rennes. These areas offer a glimpse into everyday Breton life away from the tourist crowds.

9. Seasonal Delights at Place des Lices:

Place des Lices isn't just famous for its market. During different seasons, the square hosts various events and festivals. From summer concerts to winter festivities, check the local calendar for seasonal delights and events that promise a memorable experience.

10. Rendezvous at Rue Saint-Michel:

Rue Saint-Michel is a favorite among locals for its eclectic mix of shops, boutiques, and eateries. Join the residents as they stroll down this charming street, exploring unique stores and enjoying a diverse range of culinary delights.

11. Breathe in the Greenery of Parc Oberthur:

Parc Oberthur is a local gem often overlooked by tourists. Take a leisurely stroll, indulge in a quiet moment by the pond, or simply relish the lush greenery. It's a peaceful escape embraced by locals seeking tranquility amidst nature.

12. Attend a Concert at Le Liberté:

Le Liberté is not just a venue; it's a cultural hub in Rennes. Locals recommend checking the event calendar for concerts, performances, and shows. Attending a live event here offers an immersive experience in the city's vibrant arts and entertainment scene.

13. Visit the Musée des Beaux-Arts:

While exploring Rennes, don't miss the Musée des Beaux-Arts. Locals appreciate this museum for its impressive collection of artworks spanning centuries. Take your time to wander through its halls and discover the rich cultural heritage preserved within its walls.

14. **Quiet Reflection at Saint-Pierre Cathedral:**
Saint-Pierre Cathedral is not only a historical marvel but also a place of quiet reflection for locals. Join them in appreciating the stunning architecture and serene atmosphere. The cathedral often hosts events and concerts, offering a unique blend of spirituality and cultural experiences.

15. **Join in Festive Celebrations:**
Rennes comes alive during festivals and events. Locals eagerly participate in celebrations like Les Tombées de la Nuit or the Trans Musicales. Check the local calendar and join in the festivities, immersing yourself in the vibrant spirit of Breton culture.

Local Wisdom for a Memorable Journey

1. **Learn a Few Breton Phrases:**
Locals appreciate visitors making an effort to speak a bit of Breton or French. Simple phrases like "Bonjour" (hello) and "Merci" (thank you) go a long way in fostering connections and showing respect for the local culture.

2. **Indulge in Galette-Saucisse:**

Don't leave Rennes without trying the beloved local snack, galette-saucisse. This savory delight is a Breton street food favorite and can be found at various markets and food stalls.

3. **Adapt to the Breton Pace:**

Bretons value a more leisurely pace of life. Embrace this and savor each moment. Whether you're enjoying a meal, exploring the streets, or engaging in conversations, let the unhurried rhythm of Breton life guide your journey.

4. **Be Open to Local Recommendations**:

Strike up conversations with locals, whether in a café, at a market, or in a park. Bretons are known for their warmth and hospitality, and their recommendations can unveil hidden gems and insider secrets.

5. **Participate in Community Events:**

Keep an eye out for local community events or gatherings. Joining in festivities, markets, or neighborhood activities provides a deeper connection to the heart of Rennes' community spirit.

6. **Respect Breton Traditions:**

Bretons take pride in their traditions. Respect local customs, whether it's the way food is enjoyed, greetings are exchanged, or festivals are celebrated. Immersing yourself in these traditions enhances your cultural experience.

7. Weather-Ready Wardrobe:

Be prepared for the unpredictable Breton weather. Layered clothing and a compact umbrella are handy companions. Locals often adapt their attire to the day's forecast, ensuring they can comfortably navigate the occasional rain showers.

8. Explore with Curiosity:

Rennes is a city with layers of history, culture, and charm. Approach your exploration with curiosity, and you'll uncover nuances that may escape a hurried gaze. Let each street and corner reveal its unique story.

9. Culinary Adventures Beyond Crepes:

While crepes are a Breton staple, explore the diverse culinary scene. From seafood specialties to regional cheeses, venture beyond the expected and savor the full spectrum of Breton gastronomy.

10. Capture Moments, Not Just Photos:

As you explore Rennes, let the experiences linger in your memory. While photos are wonderful souvenirs, take moments to soak in the atmosphere, engage with locals, and create lasting memories beyond what the lens can capture.

11. Connect Through Shared Stories:

Bretons love storytelling. Share your travel tales and listen to the stories locals have to tell. Whether it's a historic tidbit or a personal anecdote, these shared moments create a connection that transcends the role of a tourist.

12. **Celebrate Diversity:**

Rennes is a melting pot of cultures, thanks to its vibrant student population and diverse community. Embrace this diversity, be open to new perspectives, and you'll find that Rennes' charm lies in its eclectic mix of traditions and modernity.

Your Journey, Enriched by Local Insights

In Rennes, locals generously share the keys to unlocking the city's essence. Whether it's a hidden courtyard, a cherished tradition, or a culinary delight off the beaten path, these insights from the heart of Breton hospitality promise to make your journey truly unforgettable. With each local tip, you embark on a curated adventure, discovering the soul of Rennes guided by the wisdom of those who call it home. May your exploration be as enriching as the stories shared by the locals, and may Rennes welcome you with open arms and a treasure trove of unforgettable moments. Happy travels!

Chapter 20: Rennes in Different Seasons

The Kaleidoscope of Rennes: A Seasonal Symphony Unveiled

Seasonal Highlights

Spring: Blooms and Festivities

As winter gracefully gives way to spring, Rennes transforms into a burst of colors. Cherry blossoms paint the city with delicate hues, and parks like Parc du Thabor become radiant havens. Spring brings a sense of renewal, and locals eagerly embrace the outdoors.

Festival Mythos:

- Spring in Rennes kicks off with Festival Mythos, a celebration of storytelling and contemporary myths. The city comes alive with performances, street arts, and theatrical events, captivating both locals and visitors.

Parc du Thabor in Bloom:

- Visit Parc du Thabor to witness nature's spectacle as flowers bloom in abundance. The park's botanical beauty reaches its zenith during spring, offering a serene backdrop for leisurely walks and picnics.

Café Terrace Delights:

- Spring invites you to relish the enchanting café culture. Locals flock to outdoor terraces, basking in the sun while enjoying a cup of coffee or a leisurely meal. Places like Place des Lices become animated hubs of social activity.

Summer: Festivals and Outdoor Revelry

As temperatures rise, Rennes embraces the vivacity of summer. The city becomes a stage for various festivals, outdoor events, and lively gatherings. The long days invite exploration, with the sun casting a golden glow over Rennes' historical architecture.

Les Tombées de la Nuit:

- Summer nights in Rennes are illuminated by Les Tombées de la Nuit, a multidisciplinary arts festival. The streets become stages, showcasing theater, music, and visual arts. Join the locals in this magical celebration under the summer sky.

Rooftop Bars and Riverside Strolls:
- Take advantage of warm evenings by exploring rooftop bars with panoramic views. Quench your thirst with a refreshing drink while savoring the cityscape. Riverside strolls along the Vilaine River are particularly delightful during the summer months.

Beach Vibes at Les Champs Libres:
- Les Champs Libres transforms into an urban beach during the summer, bringing a touch of coastal ambiance to the heart of Rennes. Relax on the sandy shores, participate in beach games, and enjoy the lively atmosphere.

Autumn: A Tapestry of Colors
Autumn arrives in Rennes with a tapestry of reds, yellows, and browns. The city's parks and gardens undergo a mesmerizing transformation, creating a picturesque backdrop for autumnal walks. The cooler weather is perfect for exploring without the summer crowds.

Festival des Tombées de la Nuit d'Automne:

- Autumn hosts the Festival des Tombées de la Nuit d'Automne, an extension of the summer festivities. This autumn edition introduces a new set of performances and cultural events, adding a touch of magic to the changing season.

Fall Foliage in Parc Oberthur:

- Parc Oberthur becomes a captivating canvas of fall foliage. The changing colors of the leaves create a serene atmosphere, making it an ideal spot for contemplative walks or moments of quiet reflection.

Culinary Delights:

- Autumn brings a harvest of seasonal produce to Rennes' markets and restaurants. Indulge in hearty Breton dishes, featuring mushrooms, chestnuts, and seasonal vegetables. Cafés offer warm beverages to savor while watching the leaves fall.

Winter: Festive Charm and Cozy Evenings

Winter in Rennes exudes a festive charm, with the city adorned in twinkling lights and holiday decorations. While temperatures drop, the warmth of Breton hospitality and the festive ambiance create a cozy atmosphere.

Marché de Noël:

- The Christmas Market, or Marché de Noël, takes center stage in winter. Place de la République transforms into a winter wonderland, featuring stalls with crafts, local treats, and festive decorations. It's a perfect setting to embrace the holiday spirit.

Ice Skating at Place de l'Hôtel de Ville:

- Lace up your skates and glide across the ice at Place de l'Hôtel de Ville. The temporary ice rink, set against the backdrop of the city's historic architecture, offers a delightful winter activity for locals and visitors alike.

Festive Illuminations:

- Rennes illuminates with festive lights during winter nights. Take a leisurely stroll through the streets to admire the enchanting decorations, from the historic center to lesser-explored neighborhoods, each adorned with its unique charm.

Year-Round Gems: Timeless Rennes Delights

While each season brings its own magic to Rennes, some experiences are timeless and can be enjoyed throughout the year.

Gastronomic Delights:

- Rennes is a haven for gastronomes at any time of the year. Indulge in Breton specialties like galettes, seafood, and the renowned cider. Local bistros and restaurants offer a culinary journey that transcends seasons.

Cultural Explorations:

- Museums, galleries, and cultural spaces beckon visitors throughout the year. Whether exploring the Musée des Beaux-Arts or attending a performance at Le Liberté, Rennes' cultural scene is a constant source of enrichment.

Historic Charm:

- The historic center, with its medieval architecture and charming squares, is a perennial delight. Wander through Place des Lices, Rue Saint-Michel, and Sainte-Anne, where the city's timeless charm is woven into the fabric of daily life.

Tips for Seasonal Exploration

1. Check Festival Calendars:
- Before planning your trip, check the festival calendars to align your visit with events like Festival Mythos, Les Tombées de la Nuit, and other seasonal celebrations.

2. Layered Clothing for Autumn and Spring:
- For autumn and spring visits, pack layered clothing to accommodate varying temperatures. Comfortable shoes are essential for exploring parks and charming streets.

3. Warm Accessories in Winter:
- If visiting in winter, pack warm accessories such as scarves and gloves. The festive atmosphere and winter activities will make your stay cozy and enjoyable.

4. Plan Outdoor Activities in Summer:
- Summer is ideal for outdoor activities, rooftop explorations, and enjoying the vibrant street life. Plan your itinerary to make the most of the longer days and balmy evenings.

5. **Join Seasonal Events:**
- Embrace the local spirit by participating in seasonal events, whether it's beach activities in summer or Christmas festivities in winter. Engaging in these events offers a more immersive experience.

6. **Explore Beyond the City Center:**
- Each season offers a different perspective of Rennes, so consider exploring both the well-known attractions and hidden gems in various neighborhoods to witness the city's diverse facets.

Rennes unfolds its beauty through the changing seasons, each one adding a unique brushstroke to the canvas of this Breton gem. Whether you prefer the vibrant energy of summer, the crisp air of autumn, the floral splendor of spring, or the festive charm of winter, Rennes invites you to experience its enchanting spirit year-round. May your journey through the seasons be a kaleidoscope of unforgettable moments in this captivating city. Happy travels!

Chapter 21: Conclusion

Adieu to Rennes: A Heartfelt Farewell and Lasting Impressions

Final Thoughts

As your journey through the captivating streets and cultural tapestry of Rennes comes to an end, it's time to reflect on the myriad experiences that have painted your sojourn in this Breton gem. Rennes, with its medieval charm, modern vibrancy, and warm hospitality, leaves an indelible mark on every traveler's heart.

A Tapestry of Memories

Cobbled Streets and Historic Whispers:
- The cobbled streets of the historic center, where each step resonates with the echoes of centuries past, have woven a tapestry of memories. The medieval

architecture, adorned with flowers and street art, creates a visual feast that lingers in the mind.

Culinary Odyssey:
- The gastronomic delights of Rennes have undoubtedly tantalized your taste buds. From the comforting embrace of a galette-saucisse at a local market to the exquisite flavors of Breton cuisine in charming bistros, your culinary journey has been a feast for the senses.

Cultural Enrichment:
- Rennes' cultural scene, showcased in its museums, galleries, and performance spaces, has enriched your understanding of Breton heritage. The Musée des Beaux-Arts and Le Liberté have become portals to the city's artistic soul.

Local Treasures and Hidden Gems:
- Beyond the well-known landmarks, your exploration has uncovered the local treasures and hidden gems that define the authentic essence of Rennes. Rue Saint-Michel, Parc Oberthur, and the vibrant markets have become cherished corners of discovery.

Breton Hospitality: A Warm Embrace

Café Conversations and Smiles:

- The café culture, where conversations flow like the local cider, has introduced you to the warmth of Breton hospitality. Whether at a terrace in Place des Lices or a quaint spot in Saint-Anne, the exchange of smiles and stories has created a sense of connection.

Festivals and Celebrations:

- Rennes' festive spirit, witnessed in events like Festival Mythos, Les Tombées de la Nuit, and the Christmas Market, has become a testament to the city's vibrant energy. The shared celebrations with locals have woven a sense of camaraderie.

Nature's Embrace in Parks:

- Parc du Thabor and Parc Oberthur have offered moments of tranquility amidst nature's embrace. Whether in full bloom during spring or adorned in autumnal colors, these green havens have provided a retreat from the urban hustle.

Seasons Unfold: A Symphony of Change

Spring Blossoms and Renewal:
- Spring brought blossoms to the city, painting it with delicate hues of renewal. Festival Mythos and the vibrant café terraces signaled a rejuvenation that mirrored the blossoming flowers.

Summer's Lively Revelry:
- Summer, a season of festivals and outdoor revelry, bathed Rennes in a lively ambiance. Les Tombées de la Nuit and rooftop explorations captured the essence of warm evenings and festive cheer.

Autumn's Tapestry of Colors:
- Autumn unfolded a tapestry of reds and golds, transforming parks and streets into picturesque scenes. The Festival des Tombées de la Nuit d'Automne and fall foliage in Parc Oberthur created an atmosphere of contemplation.

Winter's Cozy Charm:
- Winter draped the city in festive charm, with the Christmas Market and illuminated streets creating a

cozy atmosphere. Ice skating at Place de l'Hôtel de Ville and festive illuminations turned the colder months into a time of celebration.

Timeless Allure:

Historic Charms and Contemporary Allure:
- The historic center, with its medieval wonders, and contemporary districts like La Courrouze have showcased the city's timeless allure. Rue Saint-Michel and Sainte-Anne have stood as witnesses to the confluence of history and modernity.

Local Wisdom and Connections:
- Local recommendations have guided your journey, providing insights into the heart of Breton life. Conversations with locals in cafés, markets, and parks have created connections that go beyond being a mere visitor.

Farewell, but Not Goodbye

Adieu to Rennes:

- As you bid adieu to Rennes, remember that the city's spirit stays with you. The laughter in café terraces, the echoes of festivals, and the timeless beauty of its streets become a part of your travel narrative.

Carry Rennes in Your Heart:
- Carry Rennes in your heart, like a well-worn map filled with cherished memories. Let the taste of Breton cuisine, the melodies of local festivals, and the images of historic squares accompany you on your journey beyond the city limits.

Farewell, Traveler
- In the final moments of your stay in Rennes, as you take one last stroll through its enchanting streets, know that the city bids you a fond farewell. Whether you leave with a piece of local art, the aroma of a Breton dish, or the echoes of a street musician's melody, may your time in Rennes be a chapter that you revisit with a smile.

As you embark on new adventures, may the lessons learned in Rennes—of savoring moments, embracing different seasons, and connecting with the heart of a city—enrich your future travels. Farewell, traveler, and may your journeys continue to be filled with the magic and warmth that Rennes has graciously shared with you. Until we meet again on the winding streets of another city, may your path be paved with discoveries and the joy of exploration. Safe travels and adieu, dear friend!

Printed in Great Britain
by Amazon